Table of Content

The theme of this chapbook is growth. The way we grow in various ways through the experiences we encounter and some of those experiences are not ours, but they still shape us.

Mellow Ballads, that move your bones is a collection of poems that contains an array of topics that are centered around the theme of growth and reflection to bring a journey of grief, love, loss, friendship, and dreams.

Within voicing my truth, I hope every reader will find the ballads that move their bones.

Love, Me

Ever ask yourself, is your love too great of a loss to give
Is your hands too small to fit every ache you live
And is your home too narrow to fit the plummeting
weight of the childhood
            you wish you missed
Because it's not a question you have ever dared to ask
yourself
You don't dare, you only dream, because you know the
shuttle only waits at the feet of dreamers
Because hope dances around you like fireflies
And you see that life is a box of treasures at your
disposal
And you cherish every gift you have ever received
Even the gift of conversational memories because you
know you can recite every feeling you ever felt for x & o
Bundle it up and throw it into the sky and call it the
falling clouds of alphabetical decay
 And k & n
 L
    M
        A
            O
But you look up to those skies and know your love lives
there
With words, with none, and in circles
You don't dare to question your tongue cursive
Because you love the language of misinterpretation,
silent communication
You want your heart to be loved like a beating poem
With rhythm and in motion, you want your lines to flow
in continuum

You want your beginnings to never end and your okies
to be oh my's
  solemn
    You know serious and you know depth
And you know that laughter flosses through the teeth of
depth because you've seen smiles in the faces of wonder
And death shatter pain and break chaos
And you know the Alpha chooses you when you turn to
choose man
Because you let your love be too great of a loss to give
and too shallow in a swarm of impatience
Because you know the wait is a ceremony of forever

        And forever always seems too late
When it comes to loving me.

Choreographed Temple

You hear the taps of the unknown call you, jingle jangles
and you don't know whether to lift your feet up or set it
down
You know that life means barefeet, set free, take a
chance
Because you stomp on concrete and you miss cracks, but
don't miss beats
Your body is a choreographed temple
You wish the messengers spoke to you the way the
lyrics do
You know the lyrics break bondage, and you don't
apologize for knowing the steps that draw you closer to
humanity
You didn't realize until then how much you love to be
spoken to and heard by grounds and creaking floors
That flying is dancing to you and spinning
uncontrollably, the way the blender spins all the tangible
fruits that are of your culture
that your loud is the whisper tunes
The unsung melodies, in your toes keys, you listen to the
noise
What it tells you to do and where it tells you to go
Your ears know the count, but still can't depict direction
You're wild
And your tamed by the notes
Structured to twist
Synchronized to turn left and right
Open your eyes and your legs become one whole
Bowing to life
Bowing to forebear
The possibility is endless when you plug into the zone
You drift and your life becomes magic to the song

Red Blazer In Inertia

chapped vermillion borders move in parables

    making out black dreams of black affection to black love scriptures.

   capitalizing adventitious fathoms, lowercasing the speeches in which rules may not apply here

but there-

he irons crinkles of crescents

  making sense of nothing :

" we are one in the same. speak life back into me as you call out my name. sweet entity,whose figure i cannot make out. for so long I've dreamt of you. your essence. purity. you run through me like a vision. sweet figment, not quite imagined. how far from what i imagined. my love for you. my love for you greater than i could have imagined. your soul,soft like the sound of your voice. words too heavy to carry on tongue. so, we speak without tongue breaking stillness. with so much to say. my ears engineered to listen. to you. i could forever. this moment fabricated in my mind, time and time again.serenity. and now i'm lost in your eyes. excuse my staring but i'm too afraid to look away. to wake. to find that this is just a vivid dream, too good to be true. how you glide through the air. your movements ring in my ears like my favorite song. the clouds must envy you. too good a story to end. my pen won't rest. ran outta paper. i began writing on my walls. maybe i've gone mad. maybe i'm crazy… about you and the way you look at me like i'm the sun and the moon or a strange balance between the two" — Jayloni

she flattens crescents

7

turning nothing into something :

we are one in the same. i see you in my soul's quest to hunt for love's fuel to fit the demands of its hunger at night. your voice is wrapped around my feeble body and for once i feel, even with my body in a deep state, i feel alive.i don't recognize every single word for it stretches across the horizons of what i have known to feel. this dream isn't real; this dream is only a dream within what my heart wants to feel. i crave the essence of your presence that never seems to have left. within the moment i called out your name, your eyes followed my echo. bouncing off the walls of your confused mind as to who I was.through this maroon fabric, i could touch you. i felt your soul on your sleeve, but it was fighting this stranger's foreign touch. and maybe you didn't know me. but you've seen me drawn across the constellations of your heart's imagination. maybe I've gone mad to feel such a way before i knew your name. maybe i made promises too early to the sky that wished I'd hale you before I'd never see you again. it's the way i looked at you, a stranger's prayer to the kingdom that writes all destiny endings. greet me and see me as i've seen you in the void of how the sun yearns for it's companion. at night where you reappeared blurred by bright shadows and coverings... crazy to have known it was you, instant as i stared at the moon. as you left passed the platform rail, i said goodbye to what was my favorite tune
  something about   p s y c h
brown filling cream smudging in to be too sweet
  you do like nutella

that sweet sweat dries her out frigid, so she reaches for
the red blazer
      but you couldn't tell her
sneaking water in to refresh his memories
  your spoon doesn't dip in the black wings of her
comforting feathers.

o s i s

that the disease of the young black naive women
fantasizes of the man who does not leave her in her
dreams, but leaves her in her reality

Queen Sized Bed

Today, I let go.
No, she let go.
She had to let go of the pain that wrapped around every
bone in her body that was holding her imprisoned
She cried so many nights
She groaned so many nights
She yearned for her mother's care
I heard it for a years entirety
I heard her every day
There was absolutely nothing I could do
I made myself believe that there was nothing
     Sorry,
  I was sorry
The only emotion that surges through my body is
apologetic
All I ever feel is apologetic
Do apologies mean anything when the person is no
longer there to receive it?
Are apologies swept up from the clouds into the wings
of those whom we can no longer see?
Everything held more importance than her
Everything holds no importance now
I squeezed onto the words of my history notes,
instead of squeezing the fingers of her shrunken hand
I put faith in the people of the past to change a letter in
my present,
than putting faith in the person in my bloodline to
change the days she could breathe just -   one more
time..
   two more times.., three more times..., fifty more

times….,
  breathe aunt
 just breathe
Suck in the oxygen, so your kids can see you just breathe
If only words were magic
If only, " Just breathe " would have been the spell
    Would it have even been the last time?
You always wanted a daughter
Use to treat me as such
Came to me at a wrong time
Where I was always angry and such
Now I am always angry
Angry at myself the most
I'm always angry for what I do
For the things I say and for the things I don't
For you will never know
I was always angry at me
Never at you
I bury my love for you at the grave that I have never left
to see
In the burying ground of the queen sized bed,
where you always use to sleep
In the soil of this poem that I have dug from my shards
underneath
Maybe we never wanted to get rid of the mattress
Because that would mean you would finally leave

Excerpt from "The Decision That Was Not Yours"

That the place in which you situated your two feet is the
mark of dying territory
And no matter how many bodies stand around you, your
body is the only one that matters
Your position is the only one that cannot flee from the
decision you did not have
From that second that will not be erased
In the place of,
deathly hollows that called you at young age
in times of sickness, sickness you did not face
could have been anyone, but it was the girl I knew of,
downed in the worst conventional way
Pounded by the blow of the confrontational human race

the hearts' of the village it took to raise us, grew less
fonder and fonder
Blamed her for standing in that corner
we wish, but
God could not have warned her
today, thou will not choose the moment, in which her
forever is not forgotten

Just remembered.

We leave this earth praying we gave it our all. We leave this earth praying we did enough to be remembered. Not idolized. Not worshipped. Just remembered.

Can that be processed amongst our commune? That one wishes from incomprehensible heights, that the echoes of their steps will travel across more than once through the hallways of their nonexistence. The sense in it all is insensible. Long live or long forgotten, to remember the ashes and dust of the decomposed is to remind oneself that I was the decomposer. That, I did eat away the flesh of my mother, my father, my friend, my lover, my sister, my brother, the stranger. I can not remember justly whom I bid farewell and the capacity of the moments tied to whom I bid farewell.
 To remember is a link to wanting, to needing, to hoping

We bid farewell praying we gave them their all. We bid farewell praying they did enough to be jubilous now. Not dazed. Not terrified. Just jubilous
 Because to fulfill the grant of their remembrance would be to vaguely mind skim through the slideshow of their life and to greatly gush in that you may never remember the hallways they stepped in

contented. Fully, contented.

Tribute to Chadwick

The movement he created through movie screens,
building a better society in our minds where we were
changing the dynamics of the arms we cross around our
hearts
Placing not one hand on our hearts looking up to white
shed stripes and the stars where we saw only their
dreams came true
So we placed two arms crossing over the W of our Will
power, screaming Wakanda Forever
    What kinda - legacy we wish to leave in each world
we become apart of forever
The kinda legacy that drives vibranium to electrify
hearts to be, on the right side of a future inclusive for
black kings and women warriors
Because when we march, when we bruise, when we push
through cemented grounds ready to fight against a cruel
system
We see, we place, and we imagine ourselves planted on
the same rich soil ground of african footprints
blossoming up the purple heart-shaped herbs where we
hear the ancestral voices telling us, " We are enough. "
They tell us to tell them, "sisi ni muhimu"
For Chadick to tell us to tell them, " sisi ni muhimu", we
are important
For the internal bleedings he felt, he bled out
homerunning legends that aimed on the basis of touching
that first base for that LA field to strike out a non
diversified sporting dystopia
Because what he made me see, was that, emerging
utopias in each discipline of our skills

We were constructing a bigger utopia where boys and girls dressed up in costumes of superheroes, to be a hero in their stories too

Because what chadwick told us is that, " villains are heroes too"

Meaning, I'm trying to save all people, but to you I'm just another enemy fighting against the unchangeable world that refuses to see me as equal

That's why he was apart of a movie representing an icon that made fair representation for all people

Because the way we were judged was more like stripped away the strength of our black panther saying, " I accept your challenge ", but there was no challenge to accept

Weaken by the solid bare front of black skin and bones

Convicted from the clicking (knck knck) heel of our toes, back to black skin tone

Guilty as charged

But for what, for what

For being the "Godfather of soul"

Chadwick also taught us funk, and soul, telling us we could find rhythm in the days we felt blue

Because we could find purpose in blue moments

We could find fire in blue times

We could find the best versions of ourselves to inspire, amongst the cracks of four years of blue days

Where cancer spread across him like a wildfire, in silence, he tied together hope like bundles of joy in his worst days

Encouraging we exercise our right to vote, before his fifteen days

Remembering my aunt and the cancer that took her last days

It's something about that colon
The way now it peaks at the charts that its a
predominantly high risk to black folks
They just noticed
Telling us now that the list that always follows after
colons, is a black name, black type, in black font, written
on a black box
Deceased
Boseman ,Chadwick
Deceased
Schmidt, Sheila
Deceased in every messed up degree that once again
Chadwick had to become our hero to shed light that
black people were dying from the colon cancer disease
He always took one for the team
Because even with no more breaths, he opened their eyes
so we could live a little bit more years than he did
He opened up their eyes so we could live to succeed
Opened up their eyes, that a big screen picture fits more
than a wakanda fantasy
More like the wakanda dream
That wealth feel betters when it's prospered from within
and distributed like grains
That competing was never the ideal way, real friendship
and the people you met along the way
Who cares about you and everything you say
Chadwick taught me that I could love the heart in every
human being because there is no telling what we will
miss hearing them say

Blessed, Together and Alone

Blessed, at my awakening you are there
to tell me good morning
I'm scared that after twenty mornings
I won't see it anymore
We are known to come close then go far
Sometimes it feels we won't make it
back in time, to make it just in time
To love each other just one last time
You want space to be sad, but you miss what we had
When I left you standing there alone
Now we are stuck in a mess, together and alone

Waffles and Words

Butter and syrup, take a bite for the first time
I have never been here, with you
With anyone, just stuffing my face with your words
Cinnamon and salt lip balm
Medicating everything to cure heartache
Naive children play in tower made recipes
Tasting and messing with the original flavors
Believing and confusing waffles with words
Sweet sweats on leveled raised anxiety
Muffles sounds of young age, old love
With my young days, remembering old words
What waffles tasted like, when you left me with no
words

Cartoons

Are you ready kids?

I was used to the sea, knowing that we live in pineapples

And make music and swallow our reads, to unplug and unsync from life as we have yet to know

Who lives in the pineapple under the sea?

That our messes aren't soaked between loose fibers of sponges and our temper-tantrums can't be blown away into air compact soap films on a large jellyfish field

Ready to find the star within us that reveals itself from under the shield of a rock

When neighbors want to sit in saunas and shade and just want us to grow up

But we still live in fantasies, hunting for formulas

Scheming with Karen's, before the name meant nothing

And everything

All at once

Not knowing what's what, where's the chum bucket and where's the treasure sanctuary

Still glued to the reality shifted on the screen

Everything is in reverse, reverse psychology

Delusionality

F is for fantasy, daring to persist

U is for you and me

N is for enchanting a hollow abyss

money hunger in the deep blue sea

If nautical nonsense be something you wish

Then drop on the deck and flop like a fish

Now we are dropped on the deck, flopping like fishes.

Dehydrated sponges and stars

*Twenty-twenty one years later... *

B,ud < 3

My beloved bud

It's a full moon tonight and I can't help but feel like the universe is smiling at me, finally. I am in a hotel room surrounded by people who came into my life at different times for different reasons. Here we sit just to be present and share this feeling together. It is a feeling that I have waited my whole life to feel. I don't know exactly what the words are to describe said feeling, but it has arrived nonetheless. I don't know why I'm writing this and I don't even know what I'm trying to say. I just want you to know that all is well and that I am here. I'm here for you like you have been for me. Thank you for listening. There is light on the other side I promise you. Don't stop dreaming, don't stop doing, and always continue. A clear mind can still be in the clouds.

Love.

Come alive. Come to me on dark evenings when you feel. Although I am too late, you were my first breath and I had loved you as such. Can I tell you the truth? Everyone, maybe? Tell everyone how our friendship was my liberation and every poem left of me written too soon. How we became one of each other and two of tomorrow when repeated that life needed you. So let's draw breath to say, " Please be my eyes and tell me everything you saw when you captured the worst of it all." Writing is mine and photographing is yours, I dream the images and you found the circles in the good news. It's terrifying for me to speak to you here, but I have waited for our time to come, for our letters to be shared, for me to say my beloved Bud. We are moving backwards in time to five years. When life was true. Truest form of meant to Be, Under Destiny. To recall thunder and championship rings and Oklahoma, forces that recollected I spoke of nothing, only you, in drunk sobriety when you knew what would end would only begin forever us, Built, Under Desire. To know me and follow my stars and leave your sky shuttered in dust blue, but I gave you my moon and you offered roses. A literal ask if roses would be good to give to a girl like me. Yes. I am accepting rose petals and want to be led down the aisle in the craters where moonrocks simultaneously flicker in our face. You were just a hologram here. My Bud in your other phase. You escaped, before I could tell you.

You were the only one I could have fell for, wholly, entirely, completely, despite your Beacon, Under Disaster

You made me love the way I wrote the alphabet in my own creation after I gave up, just you Burnishing, Up Dreams.

We Bettered, Us Daily

You were all of me. For every Bottled, Up Damage, you were bud

My favorite spoken word to speak love into, effortlessly I have never spoke of needing, effortlessly, but I wish to tell you that I need you undoubtedly

Not because you were Bud

Nor the best of my friend
But because you were
                    the best of me

We Beam Under The Horizons That Sleep, as do we

Even the sky grows restless at times.Painting the sun on its canvas for our benefit. Shedding light to the areas that crave it the most.Even then, it alternates to the midst of darker shades and cloudy illusions. Even then, the sky cannot beam bursts of happiness for each minute of every day. For the sky is our replicas, relating to our very existence in ways we fail to recognize. If nature itself cannot keep its consistency to its image, then we should call ourselves lucky to have the same inconsistency. Life, a battle of yes's and no's. Do's and don't. Hopes and let downs. Love and hate.There's too much internal wonders to keep up with. Too little time to put into process what to leave as is and what to stray away from.Too much of everything to be stuck in a compact box of small worries that will diminish at each awakening.When life hands us pain,we wrap it up in gift wrap and check the return to sender option.To endure through pain is to have our heart tell us inside that we are bigger than any giant that blocks our safe return to joy. Agony is your giant.Giants, no matter the size of their strength and the sting of their infliction. They never win. Nothing could strip away the power of your mind and the re-sparkling of the content of your soul.Just like the moon, your heart cannot stay full forever. I will glance from afar in hopes that you rekindle your amazing psyche.

The Wolverines

The goal is to get better everyday
Here, in slow motion we have learned what it's like to
better ourselves
Even if it meant losing ourselves
for a day, for a minute, between the ringing
of a passing period
I've watched time change
Here, time changed buildings
And movements, decisions, our positions
the epicenter of massive reconstruction
And even if here, time changed people -
   I'd like to think we only wanted to better ourselves
But there was a time, we opened the gates of fear and
packed purpose —
   purpose we tried to carry in suitcase backpacks
And we just smiled.

Smiled like Carebears, knocked ourselves off our feet,
and
ran through the night in a large yard in [winter
spectacular] intermission
Finding a break between tomorrow's 8am and listening
to tonight's *Tonez*
We caught our breath and ran again because if we were
tagged
We were "it"
The night's chaser, the chaser desperately trying to catch
up to one,
maybe five people at once
I'd like to think we only wanted to better—

Ourselves, for our self
But when I danced in the rain, in thunder stricken light
never counting when practice would end
When I watched a friend get stuck in her hoops trying to
fit both hands to see how wide the hoop was
How wide the hoop of curiosity gaped
When I saw a corn nut hit a teacher's eye and eyes began
to brighten, piercing through the maze of innocence
When I saw us leave the way we hadn't began, before
our time
I saw us leave it all and never look back
We left the best days of our lives
Through counting on each other like 1..2..3
we lost count
Of when the moon would fade
And we'd never be wolverines again.

Ode to Los Angeles

Do you want to go to college?

Your mom still wraps ham and american swiss cheese in
bolillos
No matter how hard the surface is at first to slice open
Because she knew inside there was a token

Texture so soft and so rich, the need to knead, in hopes it
rises
She takes a look at her child, in hopes
She, he, they   rises

Your papa, baba, carries two dangling feet near the edge
of his ears
And he hears
        the blending sound of sirens and your laughter
In the cross section of Vermont and King Boulevard
The plaza,
taking you to Payless to buy a pair of All-Star Converse
In every hallway, he hopes you don't converse in
nonsense
and know that it doesn't matter the brand of the outsoles
you wear on your feet
the sulcus in your brains are worth much more than that,
He wonders what brand will you become and represent
at the front seat

Ten years old, just size 6 youth in shoes
You're taking steps closer, yet you're still so far to
decide

To choose

Do you want to go to colegio?
At ten, they hope your answer is yes, si, shi de
At every age, they hope you continue to say yes
Knowing that in every y-e-s, you will be blessed
Because both e & s is written in success
Leaving out just the "y"

Why? Because you will be the first in generations of the
millionth generation
To see a near free higher education written in fine print
WIth names like
Castanon, Mendoza, Rodriguez, Dixon, Moore, Lagos,
Alfaro, Rivas, Andrade, Nguyen, Solis
And within that certainty, there is a solace
That in the home of soaring angels , your wings fly in
sync through the magic of each awakening day
that you will find your place
    in heights, hundreds of acres, the ceiling of lecture
halls you can't touch
But you are a vessel in the molding of the brick
structure, even if you didn't come from much
Or so you think
But El Mercadito, the heights you reach in Boyle
Heights of the walls of Gonzalez's Chicano Art
In La Placita Olvera, where the confetti blooms, ancestry
cheers to your future that has yet to start

Who do we owe our futures to

To the Saturdays, we learned what it was to be
empathetically amiable, consciously loquacious,
infatuated with language
The core of words so elongated, we dared to share with
our families the vocab lineage

To steer ahead
We were closer to catching up with the rest
Even with our disadvantages
We aimed to be the best
Because we were the scholars of Los angeles
The sensation of our family development
The residue of unfound treasure gutted out the bottom
hole
The hubs that bridge the border of our experiences
The wheels that kept arriving at Western, Jefferson,
Multnomah, and Broadway
To show up and stand out like Chewbaca on Solo's ship
Roaring our code of ethics
For our rebel alliance, defying the odds
That 62 kids had a choice
to be a trojan

A bobcat, an anteater, a bruin, a golden eagle, a wave
Becoming a new wave of fresh souls that took the
initiative in their neighborhood to grace
all the cement that is paved

For today,
when anyone ask
Do we want to go to college
We say, we made the choice

On a galaxy far far away
A while ago
To say yes

Because to whom do we owe our futures to
To the acceptances and rejection
The donors who believed in us, that we never fail to
mention
Our adversaries that may see our prosperities as a
transgression
The murals that kept us smiling at all LA intersections
Our mothers and fathers, abuelas and abuelitos advice
we had to listen to with no objections
To ourselves
Because when anyone ask do we want to go to college
We say   we did
With our nooks and public library shelf books
our minds secluded with mamba mentality
We face our reality
That today we start the road ahead
But tomorrow we begin the initiative again

To our NAI program we commend
For giving us an opportunity to answer— Yes, in our
quest

          to ascend

Author Bio

Shandela Contreras (she/her) is an alumna of Foshay Learning Center. She attended this junior high/ high school from the 6th-12th grade as a USC Leslie & William McMorrow Neighborhood Academic Initiative scholar. This program is a rigorous collegiate preparatory program that allows students to have the necessary tools to accelerate at any college. She is currently a first year at USC and is embarking on her career in Poetics & plans to dabble in the Political Science field.

A BFA in Creative Writing and a Masters in Professional Writing of Poetry is her academic goal.

In the future, she wants to become a well-known writer of poetry. She wants to create an anthology of poems from other individuals' experiences, so their journeys come to life through spoken word. Shandela plans to manage her own Center of Poetry, where people could have a safe space to write poetry and learn how to, so that their books can be published at the center and they know they have a spot on a library book shelf. Fresh contemporary voices starting from the age of 6(+) and up are what she plans to scout for because even kids have deep emotions and she wants those books to be on the front shelves. Usually people block out new authors and go to the safe books of wonderful classic authors, but she believes we need to support new voices from the beginning as well, so they don't have to wait the majority of their entire lives to be heard. It wouldn't be more so giving them an easier way out, but giving them a chance because oftentimes people say "life is short" and she always says "life is even shorter for writers." Shandela has received the Honorable Mention Award for the Los Angeles Youth Poet Laureate. She is an alumna of WriteGirls LA and the Los Angeles Times High School Insider. To name a few, her work has been featured in the anthology *Unum e pluribus,* USC NAI 2021 Gala, Emerging Writers Fellowship GetLit 2021 Ceremony.

Acknowledgments

Ever since I was a little girl, I dreamed of publishing a poetry book. I would buy journals after journals and tell those closest to me, " Make sure this gets published one day." If there was one person in the world who knew I could publish anything I was set to write, it would be the one person who wrote the first title of my life on June 29th by pushing me out into the world. She named that title, "Shandela Contreras." To my mother who knew I was a poem recreating the verses of my heartbeat and perceptions, this is for you. My tag team, my first best friend, my beautiful Olympic track star.
To my brother deme, my sister adri,my granny agnes, my dad nel, and my late grandpa sydney fun. I love you all, with my entire heart and thank you for believing in me every step of the way.

To sharmaine, tanisha, suzette, junie, rodvell, elden, adrian, kenny, chamilio, and my late sheila. There is a life I wish to give you bigger than you've ever seen and I hope I am able to one day.

To my writing mentor Ashley Bower who gave me the book, *All Along you were Blooming*. I felt I bloomed more and more through our weekly meet-ups. I hope I too can spring like Julie continuously rediscovering my love of poetry. What wonderful work you did on the series Julie & the Phantoms.

To one of my best friend's Jarred, you always told me that the poetry I presented always made you feel proud

33

of where you came from and always inspired. You are one of the reasons why I still write and when I stopped writing, you always made me hold on.

To Edward Chanking, thank you king for continuing to support my journey every step of the way.

To Jayloni, for sharing the segment of that beautiful poem included.

To the entire Foshay family and Staff, the NAI Program, friends, and The Posse Foundation. I thank you for your generosity in seeing the spark in me.

To the Writegirls Foundation and GetLit Program, thank you for giving me the power to voice my truth.

To Mila & Raul, the grooviest of all, thank you for making this fellowship worth my while and giving me a communi-tea that I will love forever.

To Alice Martinez for designing the cover, your art and your soul is magical.

To Poetry, my love and heart...

..may the ballads continue to move our bones.

Special Addition
from my Poetry Album Podcast on Spotify & Apple Podcast :

Finding Home in The Places That Glow

**Some poems that contain explicit language have been blocked out in the content of the book, but not on the apps.

The Park has no roof- Narrative Poem

 i remember i was wearing an old brown skirt, it was old, but modern. it was bold of me to go out with that on. Not because i was showing any skin, but because i was showing the attire of a fierce abolitionist, but still i wasn't free from the men that like to strip their clothes and we're supposed to call them a drunk because they travel through parks and they sit with strangers and tell them crazy stories. drunk. It's an excuse for blabber and being an egotistical jerk. i just wanted to eat free pizza and chicken alfredo and chicken bread, but you just ruined it. I thought you were a thief. i thought you stole phones, didn't know you were that type of thief. the one that goes around stealing the fun out of everything by chasing young girls, playing with pink pocket p's, and making dried up blue flannel shirts look like creep costumes. it was something about your eyes, i seen them painted on someone else I've known before. wide and stupid looking, curious but dumbfounded. *What's your name?* i didn't really know what to tell you. your eyes were too distracting, too red, too damage, too young to be out here telling me this. Said i looked like aaliyah the singer because your girlfriend look like that. you had an argument at the beach with her and that's what led you here. Cracking jokes with teenagers, except we weren't laughing. Edward was just holding it down per usual. Asking you more questions trying to keep you calm because we didn't know you like that, so why were we giving you free therapy? i keep forgetting that we were just scared, but we didn't know why yet. Until we did know why and it all made sense. You weren't just a

37

regular nobody trying to rob. Your name was masai and you think having a penis makes you a man. You make people tell you lies and play pretend. Oh yeah, I forgot Edward had to be my fake boyfriend that day. You thought you could treat me better because your names masai and you're some what?.. almighty being. Treat me better? What does " treating" mean to some people. Its jacked that you think that a slip-in is some sort of treat and i'm supposed to melt at the sight of it. i did not melt, but i ran. packed everything up because you turned a warm night - dark and stiff. you hardened at me and i hardened because of you. If i ever meet another masai, you better damn hope it's not you. drunk or sober, you are still the same maniac that couldn't keep it in your pants nor your ███ together. you are just a reminder that i was growing up. that the park won't ever look the same, neither pure or full of clean excitement. that i can't just pay attention to the slides i want to slide on, but the men that want to slide onto me. that even with green grass and big trees and bushes, it's the dirt that catches my attention. the dirt. the worms.... the masai's.

Black Feathers

It's always the same response
I don't know why I expect any different
They'll always love me but not enough to look past the
skin I wear
The bun, the braids, the shriveled curls of naturality
They miss the prime matter of importance every time, at
the cost of their own heart
I like vans and don't spend money on me
So I'm not in the shoe game, they don't call me sexy
mami
You can't see the Latina in me polished under my darker
complexity

Contreras,
 Tu hablas español ?
Un poco, pero lo entiendo mas
Es no bueno
I know it's not good

Because what good am I if the love I have to give is not
good enough for you to bypass the face that I was
offered
At birth

Chandela, Shundela, Shan, Shandy
Put it in a million forms, but the beauty is still written at
the letters to its core
I can love you more with the letters in my name and the
ones of yours
But you have to love the sound of hearing my name

Because if you don't just give me the honest truth
What is it in me that you can't love
Because if it is not me then there's something deeper
you're not telling me
It's obvious I'm brave enough
It's obvious that I care enough
It's obvious I'm not going to blatantly ask " why "
because I'm not dumb
So enough
    Give me the honest truth

Because if it is me then there's nothing else you could
tell me that I already don't know
The outer workings of me is not difficult to see than
how difficult my mind is for you to read
My invisible curves aren't flirtatious
I can't flaunt the bearings of my bottom or my bust
I have nothing to show forth but my love
I can't flatiron and turn to rapunzel, there is no pixie dust
I'm so sorry that I fell in love with you

I fell in love with the one who distracted me from
everything even the things like this
Because even I forgot
I thought you could see past what your fellow friends
would disapprove of
I thought you -
No   I thought WE could mix our cultures and make a
potion to uncast the spell of our loving devotion
To be, exactly what we already were
Everyone loves the friend in me until I'm not good
But I'm not good because all the love around me failed

In my eyes, I've seen love completely dissipate
So I told you that, " I'm falling in love with you"
But you couldn't love me, right
At least not the way I wanted you to
There was never a wrong in that
Only that you couldn't see there was a wrong, in fact
Built up the rim of lies, you couldn't disguise, you were
in need of a remedy to hide' you don't grow fond of
hazelnut seeds yet money overdrawn over cocoa puff
weed
You try to indulge in the American style that brown skin
girls don't fit your level of high
So you're elevated, on the colorism escalator
So you like nutella, but you couldn't tell *ha*
Your spoon don't dip in the black wings of her
comforting feathers
You're a different fella
And I ain't ever ever going to let your standards rain on
my umbrella
They taught us girls to never run in the rain, you slipped
and don't expect me to love the same
To the little things, I'm free to do, I chose to love you
Broaden your horizons and you could have learned a
thing or two
Thought I was the one that was trapped,
but you're scared to do you

Homegirl

I remind myself that I am much more than a homegirl. Where others can find a home in me, I want to find a home in myself. Because I am home, I'm not a homegirl. I am not the girl that will be permanent and be forced to stick to the roots that were planted long ago, so it's renters can secure comfort. I am grander than walls and wood and snap a picture and hang up because we can remind ourselves of the times-- I was home. I'm not your ████ homegirl. Stop calling me that. Stop making me that. Stop trying to come home to this girl when you want to find someone who can listen. Because I'm soundproof and everything that lives here never leaves, I became your permanent. But I'm not a homegirl. Not your homegirl. I break down and decompose. Worms that stay. Caterpillars that grow. Butterfly by day. I'm flying to the den. I'm not your homegirl, I'm finding home, boy. Not with you. You left this home   long ago.

So Love the World

I am a believer of God
But God does not believe in just good and just evil
The notion of God is not just down driven to have faith
and be good so you can enter the kingdom of heaven
Or else you will perish in the depths of hell
Its our own preservation of traditional values and to keep
a structure that we want this simplicit solution to a
chaotic equation of differences in which we have been
created
The bible must have started fairly slim with God so love
the world,
Every inch of the world, every character of the world,
and every part of the world that is beautifully unique
What is good, if the goodness of everyone is destroyed
in the quickness of an act of maliciousness
Are you good? Are we all very good?
That our sins are comparable to each other's?
And you are deserving and I am undeserving, and I am
deserving and you aren't.

My God is a good God and he knows goodness to the
bone. He knows our testimonies are heavy and they are
brittle. They come undone, they are unstructured. We
face life then we un-face it. We grace it. We break it. We
are still his children in the making.

And no child bears full goodness when they are still
curious of the things in life. Are you not curious about
anything ?

You say no, but you lie.

So does your goodness rest on your lies.

And does God not love you anyway

Go nowhere then come back

I have learned to prove myself in works and letter
grades and perhaps that is all I am worth
Why do I have to keep proving myself when I have
shown that I can make it
Is it not enough that I have made it, maybe I'll only
make it when I die and am brought back to life by the
letter F
If I fail, maybe I'll make it because then I'll have the
freedom to fail and fail again
And no one will bat an eye, because a failure always
makes it
A failure makes it to nowhere
And half the time, I don't want to be nowhere
I want to exist in the happiness of being nowhere
Not in any given space or any given time, because it is
precious to exist without having to wonder where you
are and what is it that you are meant to do at a time
Why must I exist where my time is being laid out on the
front line by someone other than myself
      Or someone other than God
God knows my worth and yet I'm still trying to prove
to the whole damn world that I can make it
When I have made it to today
But today is not enough because today doesn't make
tomorrow
   Today doesn't make tomorrow.

And you can listen to the whole damn world tell you to
do something today for the benefit of tomorrow

But doing my work today won't do my work that is for tomorrow

It'll ease the tension in your brain from today's worries but there is always tomorrow and then the tension comes right back. It refuses to leave because you got to make it.

Make the due date, make the arrival, be there, do it.
Make it, make it, make it.

I want to destroy it. Destroy the creation of making because only God can create, so why do I think I can make....

make it.

God made me wake today, so what do I have to prove
Want me to prove that my waking of today was deserving?

God so loved the world, he gave his creations the ability to think they are deserving of anyone's worth.

God so loved the world he gave me, his beloved daughter, the ability to think and spew words into rambles and lines just to prove I'm tired of making it.

But will go on trying to again tomorrow,

But will go on trying to again anyways.

Lines do touch home

No one believes in you at first
When I was in kindergarten— they told me I wrote too
B I
   G
Like big letters, off the line

Never can quite fit the space between the two parallel
lines

I mean why have the words confined to that box, am I
right?

But point is I quickly began to write in almost perfect
print
Wrote like letter typing sheet ink

I just wanted everyone to believe I could do things that
they could never think

I could ever do

Now I want to write.

I've always wanted to write poetry
Like real poetry

Like feel it poetry
Like my name is about to be called on the stage and
everyone will applaud
Because my voice means love and love defines poetry

Poetry was my first love because it believed in me
I know you think I am crazy

To believe an intangible thing that cannot speak can
possibly have the capacity to believe
But it is tangible and it does speak
Poetry speaks
It speaks through me and it can be touched
It can be touched when it reaches you

So believe in me when I tell you I want to reach you
That these words believe you

They've believed you since you have said your first
word
Since the first time they rejected you

Now you write
You are right
The believers always right, especially when the believer
is you

2461 Halloween Home

We passed by the house that looked like Christmas
during Halloween
All the purple and orange lights that spewed out in the
middle of the night
Like night trying to not be scared that the day will come
soon
All the lights and pumpkin carved spices seep into the
fading darkness and
 it was the most beautiful house I have ever seen

The car was warm and we were looking for warmth
between our eyes
Beneath the chilling night, there was a house that
haunted the streets with its glory
Not all houses were faced with the same dignity of
emotion
as the Christmas Halloween house

as the trick and the treat. Where the treat was your love
and the trick that it may not last.
he had the most beautiful heart I had ever seen

And we just stayed on the street in your 2007 honda
civic looking at that house
And I prayed the decorations would live through both
seasons
We can pretend halloween has christmas meanings

Tis the season to be jolly' Fa La La..ling more in love
with you

Made in the USA
Columbia, SC
26 November 2021

49694633R00028